Programming

Computer Programming for Beginners: Learn the Basics of C#

By: Joseph Connor

© **Copyright 2016 - All rights reserved.**

In no way is it legal to reproduce, duplicate, or transmit any part of this document in either electronic means or in printed format. Recording of this publication is strictly prohibited and any storage of this document is not allowed unless with written permission from the publisher. All rights reserved.

The information provided herein is stated to be truthful and consistent, in that any liability, in terms of inattention or otherwise, by any usage or abuse of any policies, processes, or directions contained within is the solitary and utter responsibility of the recipient reader. Under no circumstances will any legal responsibility or blame be held against the publisher for any reparation, damages, or monetary loss due to the information herein, either directly or indirectly.

Respective authors own all copyrights not held by the publisher.

Legal Notice:

This book is copyright protected. This is only for personal use. You cannot amend, distribute, sell, use, quote or paraphrase any part or the content within this book without the consent of the author or copyright owner. Legal action will be pursued if this is breached.

Disclaimer Notice:

Please note the information contained within this document is for educational and entertainment purposes only. Every attempt has been made to provide accurate, up to date and reliable complete information. No warranties of any kind are expressed or implied. Readers acknowledge that the author is not engaging in the rendering of legal, financial, medical or professional advice.

By reading this document, the reader agrees that under no circumstances are we responsible for any losses, direct or indirect, which are incurred as a result of the use of information contained within this document, including, but not limited to, — errors, omissions, or inaccuracies.

Table of Content

Introduction 7

Chapter 1 Introduction to C# 9

Chapter 2 Hello World: Writing Your First C# Program 13

Chapter 3 Understanding Data Types and Variables 21

Chapter 4 Start using if else switch Statements 39

Chapter 5 Loop Your Way around C# 49

Chapter 6 Get Introduced To Encapsulation 59

Chapter 7 Get Introduced To Classes in C# and Their Properties
.... 71

Chapter 8 A Brief on Methods 89

Chapter 9 Working with Arrays and Strings 109

Chapter 10 An Insight to Structures and Enums 129

Chapter 11 Becoming Familiar with the Concept of Inheritance
.... 141

Chapter 12 Using Constructors and Destructors 157

Chapter 13 Getting Into Interfaces and Polymorphism 165

Chapter 14 Learning the Basics of Debugging 177

Chapter 15 Tips for C# Beginners 181

Conclusion 185

Releases 187

Introduction

First of all, thank you for buying this book, "Programming: Computer Programming for Beginners: Learn the Basics of C#". C# was developed by Microsoft under its .NET initiative.

C# or C Sharp as it is pronounced is a programming language. It is a multi-paradigm programming language as it supports a variety of programming paradigms such as the object oriented discipline. As a result, you enjoy an enormous amount of flexibility in choosing a programming style for the task at hand. Moreover, C# is considered to be an easy language for beginners looking to take the first step into the huge world of computer programming.

Learning C# opens up a plethora of opportunities to you. From C#, you can take a step back and learn the incredible language of C and then C++. Knowledge of C# also enables you to pick up the skills necessary for web development through the .NET platform. Additionally, this language is also helpful if you are planning to develop products for the Microsoft ecosystem down the line.

Are you feeling overwhelmed with all of this? It might be a lot to take in for a beginner. However, you shouldn't worry too much. This book will help you get the fundamental knowledge you need to become a C# programmer. You will learn some cool new terms and even a few programs. You will come across some of the terms and functions used in this language. In short, you will be prepared thoroughly so that you can start advanced courses and become a top notch programmer.

Let us now get started on learning C#!

Chapter 1
Introduction to C#

When the .NET framework was originally being developed by Microsoft, and the programmers had to write the class libraries with the help of Simple Managed C, a managed code compiler system. However, there were a few issues with using C. As a result; C# was developed as a new language to overcome these problems.

C# has been specifically designed to be simple and modern. It is an object-oriented and general purpose programming language. If you are already familiar with programming, you will easily recognize that C# borrows a range of key concepts for a variety of other programming languages, the most notable of which is Java.

The Importance of the .NET Framework

Theoretically speaking, C# is capable of being compiled to machine code. Be that as it may, this language is almost always used alongside the .NET framework in real life. For this reason, you need to ensure that the .NET framework has been installed on the computer on which you are running the applications that you wrote in C#.

The .NET framework is compatible with a large range of programming languages. However, it is C# which is most commonly associated with this framework. It is even known as 'THE .NET language' in some circles. This is probably due to the fact that the development of the framework and the language took place at the same time.

What Do You Need To Get Started With C# Programming?

Before you get started on writing C# programs, there are a few things that you need to take care of first. Make sure that the following programs have been installed on your computer.

- The .NET Framework Software Development Kit

- An Editor

That is all. These are the only two things that you require to start programming in C#. There is a wide range of editors available. You can even use Notepad or the DOS Editor but more on that later. Be that as it may, it will be better for your learning curve if you install either one of the following optional programs.

- Visual C# .NET

- Visual C++ 6.0. This is included in the Microsoft Visual Studio 6.0 package.

Your first step should be to get the .NET SDK installed on your computer. You can easily download the program from the official website of Microsoft. You will also get a complete documentation of the program along with it. On installing this kit, you will be able to compile and execute your source code in C#. This is made possible by the Command Line Compiler that has been built into the kit along with the runtime Just in Time Compiler. If you have dabbled in Java previously, you can recognize them as being similar to the Java Compiler and the Java Interpreter, which is available in the Java Development Kit.

About the Editor

The editor is a program that is used for writing the source codes. C# is versatile in this matter as it can be written with the help of nearly any text editor. Even the basic Notepad available in Windows is a good choice. For compiling, you can easily use csc.exe, the Command Line Compiler available within the .NET framework.

When it come to developing C# programs with .NET SDK, Notepad is a popular choice. On the other hand, it is not the best editor, especially for beginners. After all, some useful features such as code numberings and syntax coloring are absent in Notepad.

That is why many developers prefer to use an Integrated Development Environment or IDE. There are quite a few options available from Microsoft, the best of which is Visual Studio. This program can be used for working on all the aspects of the .NET framework. This is certainly a highly advanced program and is available in a range of editions. The complete Visual Studio does cost quite a bit and may be too advanced even for hobbyists.

On the release of the .NET framework, Express versions of the product were introduced by Microsoft. These versions are meant for hobby programmers and those who are just starting with the .NET framework. The Express versions will only work for a single language. They may not have the most advanced features of Visual Studio, but they are free. They are also quite easy to use for learning the language of your choice which is C# in this case.

There are some other third-party editors available in the market. However, for this book, we will be using Visual C# Express for writing the code. You must remember that the codes will remain the same irrespective of the editor you are using.

Chapter 2

Hello World: Writing Your First C# Program

If you have learned or dabbled in any programming language previous to C#, you will be familiar with "Hello, world!" This is a basic example that demonstrates the programming language in action. This is exactly what you will be learning in this chapter.

This programming example will illustrate the fundamentals of the programming language. You will come across a few functions and classes that you will surely be using later while writing more advanced codes.

Starting a New Project

To start a new C# project, you should first open Visual C# Express. In the File menu, select the New Project option. The project dialog will open where you should choose the Console application. This will be the most basic application type that you can find on a system running Windows. Click on the Ok option so that Visual C# Express can create the new project for you.

You will also notice the creation of a file that has been named as Program.cs. This will be the application file where you will be writing the code. You will notice that the file already has a few lines of code as shown below.

using System;

using System.Collections.Generic;

using System.Text;

namespace ConsoleApplication1

{

  class Program

  {

    static void Main(string[] args)

    {

    }

  }

}

These lines of code will most certainly work, but the end result is nothing at all. You can run the application if you want by pressing the F5 key. This will cause Visual C# Express to compile and then execute your code. On execution, a black window will be launched which will then close again. This is simply because the application does not have any other functions to perform.

In order to make this program actually do something, you need to insert a couple of lines of code. You should enter the following two lines inside the last set of {}.

Console.WriteLine ("Hello, world!");

Console.ReadLine ();

On entering the lines, your entire program should resemble the following.

using System;

using System.Collections.Generic;

using System.Text;

namespace ConsoleApplication1

{

  class Program

  {

    static void Main(string[] args)

    {

Console.WriteLine ("Hello, world!");

Console.ReadLine ();

}

}

}

In order to run this program, you should press F5 again. If there are no mistakes, you will notice that the black window remains instead of closing. In the window, you will notice the message "Hello, world!" displayed. Of course, this is the phrase that you entered into the application.

There is a reason why C# is considered to be a very user-friendly programming language. That reason is that it is easy to understand much of the code even if you have never written programs in it before. You will easily notice this in the program that you just wrote.

Understanding the 'Hello, world!' Program

The previous application was just an example of how you can write a program in C#. Of course, you need to understand as to how it actually worked and what does the code actually mean. This is what you will be learning in this section.

To understand the program, consider the '{' and '}' first. After all, they are repeated multiple times in the program. They are known as curly braces. In C#, these braces signify the start and the end of a logical section of code. You will notice that these braces are often used in a range of other programming languages such as Java and C++ among others. As the example demonstrates, their main function is to bring together several lines of code that belong together.

using System;

using System.Collections.Generic;

using System.Text;

If you are using Visual C# Express, you will notice that the term 'using' has been highlighted in blue. This is actually a keyword, and its function is to import a namespace. A collection of classes is known as the namespace. It is the job of Classes to provide you with certain functionalities automatically.

When you are working on an advanced IDE such as Visual C# Express, the keyword, 'using' will end up creating parts of the trivial code in your stead. In this example, it was used for creating a class for you. It also imported the namespaces that are necessary or are expected to be used.

In this example, three namespaces have been imported into the program. Each of these namespaces contains some useful classes. The Console class has been used in this program, and it belongs to the System namespace.

You will also notice that the application gets its very own namespace as shown below.

'Namespace' ConsoleApplication1

This is now the primary namespace for this application. By default, any new classes created will become a part of it. It is possible to modify this and create other classes under another namespace. If you want to do so, you need to import this namespace into your application with the help of the 'using' statement.

For the next step, the class has to be defined. C# is an objected oriented language. As a result, all lines of code which actually performs something will have to be kept inside a class. For this example, the class has been named Program as shown below.

'Class' Program

It is possible to increase the number of classes in the same application. However, that was not necessary for this program. A class is capable of containing a number of methods, properties, and variables. However, that will be discussed later. In this program, there is only a single method which is declared as follows.

'Static void Main' (string [] args)

The first word of this line is static, and it is a keyword. It instructs the program to keep the method accessible without causing the class to instantiate. The void keyword tells the program what should be returned by the program which in this case is nothing.

The word, Main, is simply the name given to this method. In this case, it serves as what is known as the entry-point of the application. In other words, this will be the first section of the code that will be executed in the program.

After the name of the method has been declared, it is possible to specify a set of arguments with the help of parentheses. In this example, args is the only argument used by the method.

The next two lines are the actual program. In the first line, the Console class is used to deliver the text as output by means of the 'WriteLine' command. Of course, the text is, in this case, 'Hello, world!' The second line reads the line of text shown in the console through the 'ReadLine' command.

The ReadLine command is essential as it allows the window to remain open. Without it, the application would simply run and end. The window will be closed before you can see the output. The main function of this command is to make the application wait for some input from the user. In this example, you will find that you can enter text after the text has been displayed. On pressing Enter, the window will close and, thereby, bring an end to the program.

With this, you will have successfully completed writing your very first program. You will have also learned a few functions and terms that you are going to need while writing C# programs.

Chapter 3
Understanding Data Types and Variables

Whenever you are using a programming language, you are certain to come across data types. As C# is a strongly typed programming language, it is necessary for you to tell the compiler which data types you are going to use every time you want to declare a variable. Of course, variables are critical to any programming language.

Introduction to Data Types

In C#, data types can be broadly classified into three types. They are discussed as follows.

• **Value Type:** These data types can be directly assigned a value, and they are derived from the System.ValueType class. As such, they contain the data directly. Some examples of value types are char, Int, and Bool.

• **Reference Type:** These data types do not have the actual data kept in a variable. Instead, they have a reference to the variables. That means that they actually refer to a specific memory location. It is possible to use multiple variables to refer to a specific memory location. In this case, if one variable changes the data present in the memory location, the other variables will automatically reflect the change. Some examples of reference types include string, dynamic, and object.

- **Pointer Types:** These data types actually store the memory address of some other type. If you are familiar with C++ or C, you will understand that the pointer types in C# will have the same capabilities as that of the pointer types in those programming languages.

The Common Data Types

There are a wide variety of data types used in C#. Of course, some of them will be used more often than other when you start programming in earnest. As a result, it will benefit you greatly if you start learning about the most widely used data types. Here are some of them to help you get started.

Bool: This is one of simplest data types available as it represents Boolean value. As such, it can have only two values, either true or false. It is important to understand this type, especially when using logical operators such as the 'if' statement. By default, its value is false.

Byte: This data type represents an 8-bit integer that is unsigned. It has a range of 0 to 255 when it comes to storing numbers. By default, the value of this data type is 0.

Int: This is actually short for the integer which is a data type used for storing numbers that do not have decimals like the byte data type. However, unlike byte, Int has a range of -2,147,483,648 to 2,147,483,647. If you are working with numbers, you are more likely than not to end up using this data type.

Char: This data type represents 16-bit Unicode character, and it is used for storing only one character.

String: This can be said to be an upgraded version of the char data type as it can be used for storing text. That is, it can store multiple chars instead of a single one. In C#, this data type is immutable. In other words, after the creation of a string, they are never changed. If you use methods which can change a string, a new string is actually returned. The original one is not changed.

An Introduction to Variables

Variables are crucial to programming. In any programming language, a variable is actually a storage location which has been associated name (referred to as an identifier) and it contains some quantity of information which may be unknown or known. This information is referred to as the value. The identifier is used for referencing the stored value. During runtime, the identifier can be linked to a value, but this value may change as the program is being executed.

In C#, variables are declared in the following syntax: <data type> <name>;

However, it is possible to assign a value to the variable at the same time that you are making it visible. In such cases, you need to use the following syntax in order to do so: <visibility> <data type> <name> = <value>;

Here is an example application that demonstrates the use of variables.

```csharp
using System;

namespace ConsoleApplication1
{
    class Program
    {
        static void Main(string[] args)
        {
            string firstName = "John";
            string lastName = "Doe";
            Console.WriteLine ("Name: " + firstName + " " + lastName);
            Console.WriteLine ("Please enter a new first name :");
```

firstName = Console.ReadLine();

Console.WriteLine ("New name: " + firstName + " " + lastName);

Console.ReadLine ();

   }

  }

}

You will already recognize a few commands and statements from the earlier chapter. As such, let's concentrate on the variables.

In the program, two variables are declared first, and they have defined string type variables. A value is also assigned to the variables immediately in the same statement. Therefore, the two variables have been named as "firstName" and "lastName" and they contain the values, "John" and "Doe" respectively.

In the next statement, some text is sent as output to the console. For the output, the two variables have been used. In this case, the + characters have been used to bring together the various parts of the output text.

In the next section of the code, the user is requested to enter a new name. The input from the user is then recognized and read from the console by means of the ReadLine () method. The input is then assigned as the value of the variable, "firstName".

The next statement displays the value of the "firstName" variable to the user to denote that it has changed. This is one of the most common ways to change the value of any variable during runtime.

Now, you know the basics of data types and variables. You have also learned how to declare variables and assign values to them. You have even learned how to change a variable's value during runtime.

Converting Datatypes

Type conversion is simply the conversion of one data type to another type. Another name for this process is type casting. It is an essential part of programming. As such, it is a good idea to get familiar with it as soon as possible.

In C#, there are two different forms of type conversion as follows.

Implicit type conversion: In this case, the conversions are executed in a type-safe manner by C#. For example, converting a smaller integral data type to a larger one will be an implicit type conversion. Another example is converting to base classes from derived classes.

Explicit type conversion: These are the conversions which are performed explicitly by the users with the help of the pre-defined functions. In order to perform an explicit conversion, a cast operator is a must.

Take a look at the following example to get a better understanding of explicit type conversions.

using System;

namespace TypeConversionApplication

{

  class ExplicitConversion

  {

    static void Main(string[] args)

    {

      double d = 5673.74;

      int i;

      // cast double to int.

      i = (int)d;

      Console.WriteLine(i);

Console.ReadKey();

}

}

}

On executing the code shown above, the following result is going to be produced.

5673

The Type Conversion Methods Available In C#

There are quite a few type conversion methods that have already been built into C#.

ToBoolean: A type will be converted to Boolean value if possible.

ToByte: A type will be converted to a byte.

ToChar: A type will be converted to a single Unicode character if possible.

ToDateTime: An integer type or string type will be converted to a date-time structure.

ToDecimal: A floating point type or integer type will be converted into a decimal datatype.

ToDouble: A type will be converted to a double type.

ToInt16: A type will be converted into a 16-bit integer.

ToInt32: A type will be converted into a 32-bit integer.

ToInt64: A type will be converted into a 64-bit integer.

ToSbyte: A type will be converted into a signed byte datatype.

ToSingle: A type will be converted into a small floating point number.

ToString: A type will be converted into a string.

ToType: A type will be converted into the type specified.

ToUInt16: A type will be converted into an unsigned int datatype.

ToUInt32: A type will be converted into a long unsigned data type.

ToUInt64: A type will be converted into an unsigned big integer.

Getting a Grip on Constants and Literals

Constants are a reference to fixed values which cannot be changed in any way by the program while it is being executed. Another term for these fixed values is literals. It is possible to use any basic data type as a constant. Examples include character constants, floating constants, integer constants and string literals. Enumeration constants also exist.

The fact is constants will be treated in the same manner as that of regular variables with a major difference. That is, the values of constants cannot be altered in any way after they have been defined. Let us now take a look at each of the varieties of literals and constants.

Integer Literals

In C#, it is possible for an integer literal to be a decimal constant to a hexadecimal constant. The base will be specified by a prefix. In the case of hexadecimal constant, the prefix used is 0X or 0x. No prefix is used in the case of decimal constants.

It is also possible for an integer literal to have a suffix in a combination of L and U. L represents long integers while U is for unsigned. The suffix can be used in the lowercase or the uppercase. There are no rules about the order of the suffix.

Take a look at the following examples of integer literals.

212   /* Legal */

215u   /* Legal */

0xFeeL   /* Legal */

85   /* decimal */

0x4b   /* hexadecimal */

30   /* int */

30u   /* unsigned int */

30l   /* long */

30ul   /* unsigned long */

Floating Point Literals

These literals will be made of an integer part, decimal point, fractional part and finally, exponent part. It is possible to represent floating point literals in the form of decimals or in the exponential form.

Take a look at the following examples to get a better understanding of floating point literals.

3.14159   /* Legal */

314159E-5L   /* Legal */

510E   /* Illegal: incomplete exponent */

210f   /* Illegal: no decimal or exponent */

.e55   /* Illegal: missing integer or fraction */

If you are going to use the decimal form for the representation, you must remember to insert the decimal point or the exponent. You can even use both if you want. In the case of the exponential form, you will have to insert the integer part or the fractional part. Both can be used as well. In the case of a signed exponent, you will have to use e or E to introduce it.

Character Constants

These literals will be enclosed in single quotes. An example of a character constant is 'x.' It can be stored in a char datatype variable. A character constant need not be a plain character like 'x' always. It can also be a universal character like '\u02C0' or an escape sequence like '\t.'

String Literals

These literals will be enclosed in double quotes. Alternatively, @" can be used for the same. String constants will be containing characters that are similar to what character constants can contain. That is, they can contain escape sequences, universal characters and, of course, plain characters. If you want, you can break up a long line into several lines with the help of string literals. The parts will be separated by means of whitespaces.

Take a look at the following example. Notice that all of these forms are the same string.

"hello, dear"

*"hello, *

dear"

"hello, " "d" "ear"

@"hello dear"

How to Define Constants

Now that you know what constants are, it is time to start defining them. You will need to use the const keyword to define the constants. The syntax for constant definition is given as follows.

const <data_type> <constant_name> = value;

The following example illustrates how you can define a constant and use it in a program.

```
using System;

namespace DeclaringConstants
{
    class Program
    {
        static void Main(string[] args)
        {
            const double pi = 3.14159;

            // constant declaration
            double r;
            Console.WriteLine("Enter Radius: ");
            r = Convert.ToDouble(Console.ReadLine());
            double areaCircle = pi * r * r;
```

        Console.WriteLine("Radius: {0}, Area: {1}", r, areaCircle);

        Console.ReadLine();

    }

  }

}

After compiling and executing the code shown above, the result produced is given below.

Enter Radius:

3

Radius: 3, Area: 28.27431

Discover Nullables

There is a special data type in C# known as nullable types. It is not just the normal range of values that can be assigned to these datatypes but also null values.

As a example, a Nullable< Int32> variable can have any value in the range of -2,147,483,648 to 2,147,483,647 or it can have a null value. In the same way, a Nullable<bool> variable can have false, true or null as its value. The syntax for the declaration of a nullable type is given below.

< data_type> ? <variable_name> = null;

The following example demonstrates the use of these datatypes.

```
using System;
namespace CalculatorApplication
{
  class NullablesAtShow
  {
    static void Main(string[] args)
    {
      int? num1 = null;
      int? num2 = 45;
      double? num3 = new double?();
      double? num4 = 3.14157;

      bool? boolval = new bool?();
      // display the values
      Console.WriteLine("Nullables at Show: {0}, {1}, {2}, {3}", num1, num2, num3, num4);
      Console.WriteLine("A Nullable boolean value: {0}", boolval);
```

```
          Console.ReadLine();

    }

  }

}
```

On compiling and executing the code shown above, the following result is produced.

Nullables at Show: , 45, , 3.14157

A Nullable boolean value:

Understanding the Null Coalescing Operator (??)

This is a special operator that is used with nullable reference types and value types. The operator can be used for the conversion of an operand to the datatype of a different nullable value type operand as long as the implicit conversion is feasible. When the first operand's value is null, the operator will return the second operand's value. Otherwise, the first operand's value will be returned.

The example given below should make things easier to understand.

using System;

namespace CalculatorApplication

{

```csharp
class NullablesAtShow
{
    static void Main(string[] args)
    {
        double? num1 = null;
        double? num2 = 3.14157;
        double num3;
        num3 = num1 ?? 5.34;
        Console.WriteLine(" Value of num3: {0}", num3);
        num3 = num2 ?? 5.34;
        Console.WriteLine(" Value of num3: {0}", num3);
        Console.ReadLine();
    }
}
```

If you execute the code shown above, the following result will be produced.

Value of num3: 5.34

Value of num3: 3.14157

Chapter 4

Start using if else switch Statements

In computer programming, there are a few statements which remain more or less the same irrespective of the language you are using. There is a reason for this phenomenon, and that is these statements are crucial principles in programming. Here, you will be introduced to three of these statements.

- If statement

- Else statement

- switch statement

Understanding these statements is vital to learning to program in C# or any other programming language for that matter.

The Basics of the If Else Statements

You will find the 'if statement' in all programming languages, and it is easily the most important statement that you will find. After all, the ability to build conditional codes is a fundamental principle of developing any software. As a result, you need to be deeply familiar with this particular statement.

In C#, you will find that it is quite simple to use the if statement. In fact, you will find it very easy to use this particular statement if you have used other programming languages or are familiar with them.

One of the most important things that you need to know about the if statement is that it requires a Boolean result. In other words, the result has to be either true or false. There are a few programming languages, and it is possible to convert a number of data types into Booleans. This is not the case with C#. In this language, you have to ensure that the result has been specifically made Boolean. An example of this would be a statement like if(number). This is something you cannot use in C#. However, you can compare the 'number' to something in order to generate a Boolean result.

Even if you do not know programming, you should be able to understand the function of the else statement. It is the basics of English after all. The else statement serves as a companion to the if statement. Its job is to offer an alternative to the execution of the code when the condition stated by the if statement has not been met.

Understanding the Usage of the if Statement

In order to understand how the if statement and the else statement is used in C#, an example application can be of great help. As such, here is one such example that demonstrates the use of conditional logic in C#.

```
using System;

namespace ConsoleApplication1

{

  class Program

  {

    static void Main(string[] args)

    {

      Int number;

      Console.WriteLine ("Please enter a number between 0 and 10 :");

      number = int.Parse(Console.ReadLine());

      if (number > 10)

        Console.WriteLine ("Hey! The number should be 10 or less!");

      else
```

>   *if (number < 0)*
>
>   *Console.WriteLine ("Hey! The number should be 0 or more!");*
>
>   *else*
>
>   *Console.WriteLine ("Good job!");*
>
>   *Console.ReadLine ();*
>
>   *}*
>
> *}*
>
> *}*

As you can see, there two if statements present in this program along with their companion else statements. They have been used for checking if the number entered by the user is between 0 and 10 or not.

The code given in the example should be easy to understand. First, the user is requested to enter a number. The first if statement checks whether the number is greater than 10. If the function returns true, then a message is displayed to the user stating that the number should be less than 10. If it is false, the code proceeds to the else statement under which the second if statement is present.

The second if statement is used for checking whether the number entered by the user is less than 0. If true, a message is displayed telling the user that the number must be greater than 0. If false, the program proceeds to the accompanying else statement. This statement causes the "Good job!" message to be displayed.

Another important thing you must notice in this program is the lack of the {} characters for defining the conditional blocks of code. In C#, if a block contains only a single line of code, then the {} characters are not necessary. Do keep this mind when you are writing your own code.

The Basics of the switch Statement

In a programming language, the switch statement is akin to a selection control mechanism. It is generally used to let the value of a variable modify the control flow of the program execution by means of a multiway branch. Think of the switch statement as a set of multiple if statements.

The switch statement will list a number of possibilities, and each possibility will have its own action. There will also be a default action which will be taken if no other possibility is returned as true. Just like the if statement is accompanied by the else statement, the switch statement has a companion in the form of the case statement. However, multiple case statements have to be used with a single switch statement unlike if else statements.

Take a look at the following blocks of code to get a better understanding of switch statements. The example given below contains one of the simplest implementations of the switch statement.

Int number = 1;

switch (number)

{

   case 0:

      Console.WriteLine ("The number is zero!");

      break;

   case 1:

      Console.WriteLine ("The number is one!");

      break;

}

As you can see, the identifier that has to be checked is placed after the switch keywords. This is followed by a list of case statements. These statements check the identifier against a specific value.

You must have noticed that a break statement has been added to each case. This is due to the requirements of the programming language. In C#, the block has to be left before it comes to an end. If a function was being written, a return statement could have been used in the place of the break statement.

The given example makes use of an integer. However, it is possible to use any simple data type with the switch statement. Additionally, the same action can be specified for multiple case statements.

Understanding the Usage of the Switch Statement

Of course, the best way to understand how the switch case statements are used is through an example. The following example will illustrate how switch statements are applied with the case statements. It also highlights the default action capability of switch statements.

Console.WriteLine ("Is C# easy ? (yes/no/maybe)");

string input = Console.ReadLine();

switch (input.ToLower())

{

  case "yes":

  case "maybe":

    Console.WriteLine ("Awesome!");

    break;

```
    case "no":

        Console.WriteLine ("Let's try harder!");

        break;

    default:

        Console.WriteLine ("I'm sorry, I don't understand that!");

        break;
}
```

As you can see in the application, the user is asked a question and then requested to provide an answer on the basis of the options given. There are three options, and they are yes, no and maybe. The user has to choose one option and types it. The user input is then read by the application and this input then proceeds to the switch statement.

The statement switch (input.ToLower ()) is used for converting the input into the lowercase to simplify the application and make it friendlier to the user. After all, the user will not have to be requested to provide the input in lowercase.

The switch case statements proceed as follows. The user would be shown the "Awesome!" message if the input was "yes" or "maybe". If the input were "no", the message would display "Let's try harder!" to the user.

However, it is certainly possible that the user ends up making a typing mistake. It is also possible that the user writes something that is not one of the given options. In these cases, the switch statement would not generate any output whatsoever if the default keyword was not mentioned. Since it is present in this application, the program will return "I'm sorry, I don't understand that!"

The job of the default statement is to provide an alternative action if all of the case statements turn out to be false. Of course, this is a completely optional statement but useful in many circumstances nonetheless.

You should have become family with the functions of these statements and how they are meant to be used. You should now be able to implement the if else statements and the switch case statements easily into your codes.

Chapter 5
Loop Your Way around C#

When you are writing software or applications, you will need to use Loops. This is an essential technique prevalent in all programming languages. A loop can be defined as a sequence of instructions which are repeated continually till a certain predefined condition is met. In simple terms, a block of code is repeated a set number of times till a condition are fulfilled.

Generally in a loop, a certain process is performed. This can be as simple as fetching a specific data item and modifying it. After it, a condition is checked. For example, a counter can be checked to see if it has reached a specific number. If the number has not been reached, the next instruction for the program is to return to the very first instruction of the sequence. As such, the sequence is repeated. Once the condition has been fulfilled, the instruction will cause the program to proceed to the next set of sequential instructions. It can also branch out from the loop.

There is a special kind of loop known as an infinite loop. In this loop, there is an absence of a functioning exit instruction. As a result, the loop will repeat continually till it is sensed by the operating system which will terminate the program and an error will show. The infinite loop can also be stopped due to the occurrence of some other event. For example, the program can be made to terminate automatically after a specific duration of time.

In C#, you will come across four different kinds of loops. As such, you need to be familiar with them.

The while Loop

The simplest of the four loops in C# is the while loop. In this type of loop, a sequence of instructions will be executed continually as long as the defined condition returns true. It will only exit when the condition returns false. Here is an example to help you understand it.

using System;

namespace ConsoleApplication1

{

   class Program

   {

     static void Main(string[] args)

     {

```
        Int number = 0;

        while (number < 10)

        {

            Console.WriteLine (number);

            number = number + 1;

        }

        Console.ReadLine ();

    }

  }

}
```

When you run this code, you will find that the program lists a sequence of numbers in the console starting at 0 and ending at 10.

Of course, the variable number is first defined as 0. Every time the loop is executed, the variable is incremented by 1. You can see this happening in this statement:

number = number + 1

As a result, the program keeps displaying the numbers till it reaches nine which is the last thing to be displayed. You may be wondering why nine is being displayed when you have mentioned 10 in the code.

The condition will only be true when the number is less than 10. Once the number becomes 10, the condition becomes false. After all, ten is not less than 10. As you can see, the condition of the while loop is checked before the program enters the loop sequence. Once the number turns 10, the condition becomes false, and the while loop sequence is not executed.

The do Loop

The do loop shares certain similarities with the while loop with one major difference. The while loop checks the condition before the loop sequence is executed. On the other hand, the do loop will check the condition after the loop has been executed. This means the loop sequence will always be executed at least one time before exiting. This is not possible with the while loop. Take a look at the following example.

using System;

namespace ConsoleApplication1

{

  class Program

  {

    static void Main(string[] args)

```
{
    Int number = 0;
    do
    {
        Console.WriteLine (number);
        number = number + 1;
    } while (number < 10)
    Console.ReadLine ();
    }
  }
}
```

On running this program, you will see the numbers being displayed from 0 to 9. Once the number becomes 10 or more than 10, the program will exit the loop sequence. As you can see, the do loop functions in a similar manner to the while loop but checks the condition after the execution of a sequence.

The for Loop

The for loop is different from that of the do or the while loops. The for loop is generally used when you know the exact number of iterations that you want. It can also be used when you have defined a variable that contains the amount. The following example illustrates the use of the for loop.

using System;

namespace ConsoleApplication1

{

  class Program

  {

    static void Main(string[] args)

    {

      Int number = 10;

      for (Int i = 0; i < number; i++)

        Console.WriteLine (i);

      Console.ReadLine ();

    }

  }

}

When running this program, you will find that the output is the same as that of the previous examples. However, the for loop tends to be more compact than the while, and the do loops, as you can see.

There are three parts to the for loop. First, a variable is initialized for counting. Then, a conditional statement is defined to test the variable. Finally, we increment the counter variable. In C# and a few other programming languages, you can use ++ instead of writing the entire statement: "variable = variable + 1" The result will be the same.

The first section will be executed only once before the actual loop starts. This is the section where the variable i is defined and then set to 0. The next two sections will be executed for each iteration of the for loop. In each repetition, the variable I will be compared to the number variable. When the variable i is less than the number variable, the loop will run once again. After the execution, the variable I will be increased by 1. In this case, it will continue to loop till variable I become equal to 10.

The for each Loop

The for each loop is quite different from the previous three loops. This loop operates on a collection of items. Arrays or other kinds of built-in list types can also be used. For the following example, an ArrayList is used as it is one of the simple lists available in C#. ArrayList tends to work in a similar to an array.

using System;

```csharp
Using System.Collections;
namespace ConsoleApplication1
{
    class Program
    {
        static void Main(string[] args)
        {
            ArrayList list = new ArrayList ();
            list.Add ("Dog");
            list.Add ("Cat");
            list.Add ("Bird");
            foreach (string name in list)
                Console.WriteLine (name);
            Console.ReadLine ();
        }
    }
}
```

As you can see, an instance of an ArrayList is created first in the code. This is followed by the addition of a few string items to the list. In this example, we have added a few names of animals as string items to the ArrayList list.

The foreach loop is then used to run through each of the items. In each repetition, the name variable is set to the item that has been reached in the ArrayList. This variable is then pushed for output. As a result, you can see the animals that were inserted into the ArrayList being displayed on the console

It is vital that you inform the foreach loop as to which data type you are looking to take out of the collection. In this case, we have specified that the name variable will belong to the string data type. It is possible that you have a list of different data types. In such cases, you can use the object class rather than a specific class so as to take out each item of the list as an object.

If you are going to be using collections in your programs, you will find the foreach loop to be the best choice among all the loop types available in C#. This is mainly because the foreach is simpler than all of the other loops when it comes to such operations.

Chapter 6

Get Introduced To Encapsulation

There are four fundamental concepts in object oriented programming. They are an inheritance, abstraction, polymorphism, and encapsulation. As a result, you are certain to come across encapsulation when programming in C#. So, let us learn about it now so that the advanced courses become easier when you opt for them.

What Is Encapsulation?

Encapsulation can be explained as the process of which one or more items can be enclosed inside a physical or a logical package. In OOP methodology, encapsulation can prevent access to the implementation details.

In object oriented programming, encapsulation and abstraction are related features. With abstraction, it is possible to make the relevant information visible. On the other hand, encapsulation will allow the user to implement abstraction at the level desired.

Access specifiers are used in order to implement encapsulation. Access specifiers will be defining the scope and the visibility of the class member. In C #, support for the given access specifiers will be provided.

- Public
- Protected
- Private
- Internal
- Protected internal

We will be taking a look at each of these access specifiers in turn.

Public Access Specifier

This specifier will allow a class to expose the member functions and member variables to the other functions as well as objects. It is possible to access any public member from the outside of its class.

Take a look at the following example for getting a better grasp over public access specifiers.

using System;

namespace RectangleApplication

{

```csharp
class Rectangle
{
    //member variables
    public double length;
    public double width;
    public double GetArea()
    {
        return length * width;
    }
    public void Display()
    {
        Console.WriteLine("Length: {0}", length);
        Console.WriteLine("Width: {0}", width);
        Console.WriteLine("Area: {0}", GetArea());
    }
}//end class Rectangle
class ExecuteRectangle
{
```

```
static void Main(string[] args)
{
    Rectangle r = new Rectangle();
    r.length = 4.5;
    r.width = 3.5;
    r.Display();
    Console.ReadLine();
}
}
}
```

The following result will be produced once you execute the code shown above.

Length: 4.5

Width: 3.5

Area: 15.75

In the above example, notice that the member variables width and length are declared as public. As a result, it is possible to access them from the function Main() with an instance, named r, of the Rectangle class. Moreover, the member functions,

GetArea() and Display(), can also access those variables directly without the use of any instance of the class. Display(), the member function has also been declared public. This allows it to be accessed as well from Main() with the instance r of the Rectangle class

Private Access Specifier

With this specifier, a class can hide the member functions and member variables from the other objects and functions. Only the functions belonging to the same class can access the private members. It is not even possible for an instance of class to access the private members.

The example given below illustrates the concept of private access specifiers.

using System;

namespace RectangleApplication

{

  class Rectangle

  {

   //member variables

   private double length;

   private double width;

```csharp
   public void Acceptdetails()
   {
      Console.WriteLine("Enter Length: ");
      length = Convert.ToDouble(Console.ReadLine());
      Console.WriteLine("Enter Width: ");
      width = Convert.ToDouble(Console.ReadLine());
   }
   public double GetArea()
   {
      return length * width;
   }
   public void Display()
   {
      Console.WriteLine("Length: {0}", length);
      Console.WriteLine("Width: {0}", width);
      Console.WriteLine("Area: {0}", GetArea());
   }
}//end class Rectangle
```

```
class ExecuteRectangle
{
    static void Main(string[] args)
    {
        Rectangle r = new Rectangle();
        r.Acceptdetails();
        r.Display();
        Console.ReadLine();
    }
}
}
```

On executing the code shown above, the following result is produced.

Enter Length:

4.4

Enter Width:

3.3

Length: 4.4

Width: 3.3

Area: 14.52

In the example shown above, you will have noticed that the member variables width and length have been declared private. Therefore, it is not possible to access them from the function Main(). Only the member functions Display() and AcceptDetails() can access those variables. As these member functions have been declared public, it is possible to access them from Main() with the instance r of the Rectangle Class.

Protected Access Specifier

This specifier will enable a child class to get access to the member functions and member variables of the base class. As a result, the specifier is useful in the implementation of inheritance.

Internal Access Specifier

This specifier will permit a class to expose its member functions and member variables to the other objects and functions in the current assembly. That is to say, a member with an internal access specifier is accessible from any method or class that has been defined within the application in which that member has been defined.

Take a look at the following example to get a better understanding of this specifier.

```csharp
using System;
namespace RectangleApplication
{
  class Rectangle
  {
    //member variables
    internal double length;
    internal double width;
    double GetArea()
    {
      return length * width;
    }
    public void Display()
    {
      Console.WriteLine("Length: {0}", length);
      Console.WriteLine("Width: {0}", width);
```

```csharp
            Console.WriteLine("Area: {0}", GetArea());
    }
}//end class Rectangle


class ExecuteRectangle
{
    static void Main(string[] args)
    {
        Rectangle r = new Rectangle();
        r.length = 4.5;
        r.width = 3.5;
        r.Display();
        Console.ReadLine();
    }
 }
}
```

On executing the above code, the following result is achieved.

Length: 4.5

Width: 3.5

Area: 15.75

As you will notice in the example, GetArea() has not been declared with any access specifiers. If an access specifier has not been mentioned, the class member will be given the default access specifier of private.

Protected Internal Access Specifier

This access specifier allows the class to make its member functions and member variables hidden from the other class functions and objects. Only the child classes, if any, within the same application will get access to those members. This access specifier is often used in the implementation of inheritance.

Chapter 7

Get Introduced To Classes in C# and Their Properties

As you can recall, C# is an object oriented programming language. If you know a bit of computer programming, you will have certainly heard of classes. Classes are absolutely vital in object oriented programming.

A class can be said to be a construct with which you can build custom types by bringing together variables of different types, events and methods. A class, in other words, is a group which contains variables and methods which are related together. A class will be describing in these things. In the majority of cases, you will be creating an instance of the class will be referred to as the object. You can use the defined variables and methods on this object. It is certainly possible to create multiple instances of the class as per the requirements of your code.

Understanding Classes

You will have already come across the use of classes in the previous examples. After all, anything you build in C# will have to be built on classes. A better understanding can be gained by use of the following example.

using System;

namespace ConsoleApplication1

{

  class Program

  {

    static void Main(string[] args)

    {

      Car car;

      car = new Car("Red");

      Console.WriteLine (car.Describe ());

      car = new Car("Green");

      Console.WriteLine (car.Describe ());

      Console.ReadLine ();

    }

}

class Car

{

   private string color;

   public Car(string color)

   {

      this.color = color;

   }

   public string Describe()

   {

      return "This car is " + Color;

   }

   public string Color

   {

      get { return color; }

      set { color = value; }

   }

}

}

As you can see, a new class has been defined first and has been named as Car. To make it easier, the class has been declared alongside the main application in the same file. Generally, new classes tend to be defined in their very own files, however,

A single variable has also been defined and is called color. Moreover, it has been declared as a private variable. This is something that you should keep in mind. A property should generally be used for accessing variables from outside. At the end of the Car class, the Color property has been defined. This allows the color variable to be accessed.

A constructor has also been defined by the Car class and it is taking a parameter. This allows us to use a color to initialize the Car objects. As there is a single constructor in this application, only a color can be used for instantiating the Car objects.

The Describe () method has also been used. Its purpose is to allow the users to enjoy some extra text along with the information that has been recorded. It will only return a string along with the data that has been provided.

In the primary application, a variable has been declared, and it is of the type Car. This is followed by the creation of a new instance keeping the parameter as "Red". As per the coding of the class, the color red is going to be allocated as the car's color.

In order to verify that this is the case, the Describe () method is used again.

The same steps are performed once again in order to show you that it is actually quite easy to create multiple instances of the same class. Of course, another color has been used this time around.

Understanding Properties of a Class

The job of properties is to enable you to control how accessible the variables of a class are. Properties are always the recommended way for accessing the variables from outside in any object oriented programming languages. You will have already come across the use of properties in the previous example.

A property can be said to be a combination of a method and a variable. As such, it cannot take any parameters. On the other hand, the value can be processed before it is assigned to be returned. A property will consist of two sections. There will be a get method and a set method. Both of them will be taken together inside the property. You can see an example of this in the following code.

private string color;

public string Color

{

get { return color; }

set { color = value; }

}

The get method must be used for returning the variable. On the other hand, the set method must be used for assigning a value to that variable. Of course, the above example is a very simple example of a code involving a property. As such, it is certainly possible to extend it further.

There is another thing that you should understand about properties. A property requires at least one method to work. In other words, you can use either a get method or a set method. The other method becomes optional in these cases. This technique allows you to define read-only properties or write-only properties as per your requirements.

Here is another example that further illustrates the potential of properties.

public string Color

{

  get

  {

    return color.ToUpper();

```
    }
  set
  {
    if (value == "Red")
      color = value;
    else
      Console.WriteLine ("This car can only be red!");
  }
}
```

As you can see, this a more complex piece of code featuring a more advanced property. Now, you will find that the color variable is going to be returned in only uppercase characters. This is due to the addition of the ToUpper () method to the variable before it is returned. The next section of the code will set the color variable. However, the only value that will be accepted is "Red".

A Short Guide to Visibility

Throughout this guide, you will have come across the terms public and private. You may have been wondering as to what they stand for. Well, they are keywords that denote the visibility of the item in question.

The visibility of any item determines how open that item is. Visibility can be applied to a class, a property, a variable or even a method. The most common types of visibility are private visibility and public visibility. However, C# has a number of other types of visibility, all of which are mentioned below. Of course, not all of them are going to be useful for you at this stage, but you are certain to come across them as your advance in C#.

- **Public:** An item defined as the public can be reached from all places this is the least restrictive of all the types of visibilities. By default, items like Interfaces and Enums have public visibility.

- **Private:** This visibility is the most restrictive of all the types of visibilities. The private items can only be accessed by other items from the same class. By default, structs and classes are set to being privately visible.

- **Internal:** These items can only be accessed from inside the same project.

- **Protected:** Items designated as protected can be accessed only from inside the same class or from a class that inherits from that class.

- **Protected internal:** This visibility is similar to internal visibility but with a major difference. Classes that inherit from the class of the protected internal item can access that item even if the inherited classes are present in another project.

You should now be able to create simple classes on your own and even create their properties. Of course, this is only the basic level. With practice and further knowledge, you can create incredibly complex and awesome programs featuring multiple classes and properties.

Getting a Grip on Member Functions and Encapsulation

In class, a member function is a function which has its prototype or definition within the class definition in a similar manner to other variables. A member function can operate on any object of its class. It also has access to each and every member of the class for that object.

On the other hand, member variables are attributes for an object. As such, they will be kept private in order to implement encapsulation. They can only be accessed by use of the public member functions.

The following example illustrates the use of class members. Here, the value of the different class members is being sought.

using System;

namespace BoxApplication

{

```
class Box
{
  private double length;   // Length of a box
  private double breadth;  // Breadth of a box
  private double height;   // Height of a box
  public void setLength( double len )
  {
    length = len;
  }
  public void setBreadth( double bre )
  {
    breadth = bre;
  }
  public void setHeight( double hei )
  {
    height = hei;
  }
  public double getVolume()
```

```
    {
        return length * breadth * height;
    }
}
class Boxtester
{
    static void Main(string[] args)
    {
        Box Box1 = new Box();   // Declare Box1 of type Box
        Box Box2 = new Box();
        double volume;
        // Declare Box2 of type Box
        // box 1 specification
        Box1.setLength(6.0);
        Box1.setBreadth(7.0);
        Box1.setHeight(5.0);
        // box 2 specification
        Box2.setLength(12.0);
```

```
      Box2.setBreadth(13.0);

      Box2.setHeight(10.0);

      // volume of box 1

      volume = Box1.getVolume();

      Console.WriteLine("Volume of Box1 : {0}" ,volume);

      // volume of box 2

      volume = Box2.getVolume();

      Console.WriteLine("Volume of Box2 : {0}", volume);

      Console.ReadKey();
   }
 }
}
```

On executing the code given above, the following result will be produced.

Volume of Box1 : 210

Volume of Box2 : 1560

Static Members of a Class in C#

Class members can be defined as static with the help of the static keyword. On declaring a specific member of the class as static, there will only be a single copy of that static member irrespective of the number of objects created for that class.

In other words, the static keyword denotes that only a single instance of that member will exist for a class. Static variables tend to be used in defining constants. This is due to the fact that it is possible to retrieve their values by invoking the class without the creation of an instance. The initialization of static variables can take place outside the class definition or member function. At the same time, static variables can be initialized inside the class definition.

Take a look at the following example.

```
using System;

namespace StaticVarApplication
{
  class StaticVar
  {
    public static int num;
    public void count()
    {
      num++;
```

```
    }
    public int getNum()
    {
        return num;
    }
}
class StaticTester
{
    static void Main(string[] args)
    {
        StaticVar s1 = new StaticVar();
        StaticVar s2 = new StaticVar();
        s1.count();
        s1.count();
        s1.count();
        s2.count();
        s2.count();
        s2.count();
```

        Console.WriteLine("Variable num for s1: {0}", s1.getNum());

        Console.WriteLine("Variable num for s2: {0}", s2.getNum());

        Console.ReadKey();

    }

  }

}

The following result is produced when you execute the code shown above.

Variable num for s1: 6

Variable num for s2: 6

A member function can also be declared as static. These functions will be accessed static variables only. Moreover, static functions can exist even before the creation of the object.

Take a look at the following example to get a better understanding of these static functions.

using System;

namespace StaticVarApplication

{

```
class StaticVar
{
    public static int num;
    public void count()
    {
        num++;
    }
    public static int getNum()
    {
        return num;
    }
}
class StaticTester
{
    static void Main(string[] args)
    {
        StaticVar s = new StaticVar();
        s.count();
```

```
        s.count();

        s.count();

        Console.WriteLine("Variable num: {0}", StaticVar.getNum());

        Console.ReadKey();
    }
  }
}
```

On compiling and executing the above code, you will find the following result to be produced.

Variable num: 3

Chapter 8
A Brief on Methods

As you have been reading this book, you will have come across methods more than once. If you were wondering what they are, well, this is where you get to know about them. Methods are one of the basic things about programming that you should know about.

What is a Method?

A method can be said to be a group of statements that can perform a task together. All programs in C# will have one class at the very least that contains a method with the name of Main. You will have already come across them.

In order to use a method, the method will have to be defined first. Then, the method will be called. Let's take a look at each of this process.

Defining a Method

When a method is defined, the elements of the method's structure are declared. The syntax for defining a method in the C# language is given as shown.

<Access Specifier> <Return Type> <Method Name>(Parameter List)

{

  Method Body

}

A method can have various elements. They are mentioned as follows.

Access Specifier: As you already know, the access specifier will determine the visibility of a method or a variable from another class.

Return Type: It is possible for methods to return values. The return type states the datatype of the value that will be returned by the method. If there are no values being returned by the method, then the return type will be void.

Method name: This is the unique identifier of the method name. The name is case sensitive. Moreover, the identifier cannot be the same as any of the other identifiers that have been declared in the class.

Parameter list: The parameters are what are used for passing and receiving data from methods. They are enclosed in parentheses. The parameter list will refer to the order, number and type of parameters of the method. Importantly, it is possible for a method not to have any parameters.

Method Body: The body will contain the set of instructions that is necessary for the completion of the activity.

Take a look at the example given below. In this snippet of code, you will notice a function FindMax. It takes two integer values and compares them. The larger of the values will be returned. The function has a public access specifier. Therefore, it is accessible from the outside of the class by using an instance of it.

class NumberManipulator

{

  public int FindMax(int num1, int num2)

  {

    / local variable declaration */*

    int result;

    if (num1 > num2)

      result = num1;

    else

         result = num2;

      return result;

   }

...

}

Calling a Method

In C#, it is quite easy to call a method as it can be done just by using its name. Take a look at the example given below. It shows how a method is called.

using System;

namespace CalculatorApplication

{

   class NumberManipulator

   {

      public int FindMax(int num1, int num2)

      {

         /* local variable declaration */

         int result;

         if (num1 > num2)

```
      result = num1;
   else
      result = num2;
   return result;
}
static void Main(string[] args)
{
   /* local variable definition */
   int a = 100;
   int b = 200;
   int ret;
   NumberManipulator n = new NumberManipulator();
   //calling the FindMax method
   ret = n.FindMax(a, b);
   Console.WriteLine("Max value is : {0}", ret );
   Console.ReadLine();
}
}
```

}

On executing the code shown above, the following result is produced.

Max value is : 200

It is possible to call a public method from the other classes simply by using an instance of the method's class. The example given below shows you how. In this case, the method FindMax is a part of the class NumberManipulator. It can be called from another class named Test.

using System;

namespace CalculatorApplication

{

  class NumberManipulator

  {

    public int FindMax(int num1, int num2)

    {

      /* local variable declaration */

      int result;

      if(num1 > num2)

```
      result = num1;
   else
      result = num2;
   return result;
  }
}
class Test
{
  static void Main(string[] args)
  {
    /* local variable definition */
    int a = 100;
    int b = 200;
    int ret;
    NumberManipulator n = new NumberManipulator();
    //calling the FindMax method
    ret = n.FindMax(a, b);
    Console.WriteLine("Max value is : {0}", ret );
```

             Console.ReadLine();

    }

  }

}

The result given below is produced by the above example.

Max value is : 200

Understanding Recursive Method Call

It is possible for a method to call itself. Such a process is called recursion. The following example illustrates the use of a recursive method call. Here, a factorial is calculated for a given number with the help of a recursive method call.

using System;

namespace CalculatorApplication

{

  class NumberManipulator

  {

    public int factorial(int num)

    {

      /* local variable declaration */

```csharp
   int result;
   if (num == 1)
   {
      return 1;
   }
   else
   {
      result = factorial(num - 1) * num;
      return result;
   }
}


static void Main(string[] args)
{
   NumberManipulator n = new NumberManipulator();
   //calling the factorial method
   Console.WriteLine("Factorial of 6 is : {0}", n.factorial(6));
   Console.WriteLine("Factorial of 7 is : {0}", n.factorial(7));
```

Console.WriteLine("Factorial of 8 is : {0}", n.factorial(8));

Console.ReadLine();

   }

 }

}

On compiling and executing the code shown above, the following result is produced.

Factorial of 6 is: 720

Factorial of 7 is: 5040

Factorial of 8 is: 40320

How to Pass Parameters to a Method?

If you call a method that has parameters, the parameters will have to be passed to the method. There are three ways that you can pass parameters to a method. We will take a look at each of them in turn.

Value Parameters

Passing the parameters by their value is the default mechanism when parameters need to be passed to a method. In this case, a new storage location will be created for each of the value parameters when the method is called. Then, the values of the original parameters will be copied into them. Any changes made to the parameter while inside the method is not going to affect the argument.

Take a look at the example given below.

```
using System;

namespace CalculatorApplication
{
    class NumberManipulator
    {
        public void swap(int x, int y)
        {
            int temp;

            temp = x; /* save the value of x */
            x = y;    /* put y into x */
            y = temp; /* put temp into y */
        }
        static void Main(string[] args)
        {
```

```
      NumberManipulator n = new NumberManipulator();
      /* local variable definition */
      int a = 100;
      int b = 200;
      Console.WriteLine("Before swap, value of a : {0}", a);
      Console.WriteLine("Before swap, value of b : {0}", b);
      /* calling a function to swap the values */
      n.swap(a, b);
      Console.WriteLine("After swap, value of a : {0}", a);
      Console.WriteLine("After swap, value of b : {0}", b);
      Console.ReadLine();
   }
 }
}
```

The following is the result of executing the code shown above.

Before swap, value of a :100

Before swap, value of b :200

After swap, value of a :100

After swap, value of b :200

Reference Parameters

This is a reference to a variable's memory location. When using this mechanism, a new storage location will not be created for the parameters unlike what happens with value parameters. Reference parameters will represent the exact memory location of the actual parameters which have been supplied to the method. It is possible to declare the reference parameters with the help of the ref keyword.

Look at the following example.

using System;

namespace CalculatorApplication

{

  class NumberManipulator

  {

    public void swap(ref int x, ref int y)

    {

      int temp;

      temp = x; /* save the value of x */

      x = y;   /* put y into x */

```
      y = temp; /* put temp into y */
   }

   static void Main(string[] args)
   {
      NumberManipulator n = new NumberManipulator();
      /* local variable definition */
      int a = 100;
      int b = 200;
      Console.WriteLine("Before swap, value of a : {0}", a);
      Console.WriteLine("Before swap, value of b : {0}", b);
      /* calling a function to swap the values */
      n.swap(ref a, ref b);
      Console.WriteLine("After swap, value of a : {0}", a);
      Console.WriteLine("After swap, value of b : {0}", b);
      Console.ReadLine();
   }
}
```

}

Upon executing the code shown above, the following result is produced.

Before swap, value of a : 100

Before swap, value of b : 200

After swap, value of a : 200

After swap, value of b : 100

As you can see, the values present in the swap function have been changed. This alteration is reflected in the Main function.

Output Parameters

A return statement is capable of returning only a single value from a function. Be that as it may, it is possible to return two values with the help of output parameters from a function. The fact is that output parameters are rather similar to the reference parameters. There is a major difference, however. Output parameters are capable of transferring data out of the given method instead of into it.

The example given below shows the use of output parameters.

using System;

namespace CalculatorApplication

{

```
class NumberManipulator
{
   public void getValue(out int x )
   {
      int temp = 5;
      x = temp;
   }
   static void Main(string[] args)
   {
      NumberManipulator n = new NumberManipulator();
      /* local variable definition */
      int a = 100;

      Console.WriteLine("Before method call, value of a : {0}", a);
      /* calling a function to get the value */
      n.getValue(out a);
      Console.WriteLine("After method call, value of a : {0}", a);
```

```
        Console.ReadLine();

    }

  }

}
```

After you execute the code shown in the example above, the following result will be produced.

Before method call, value of a : 100

After method call, value of a : 5

For the output parameter, the variable supplied does not require a value to be assigned to it. As such, output parameters are quite useful when you have to return the values from a method by means of the parameters without getting an initial value assigned to the parameter.

This is demonstrated in the following example.

```
using System;

namespace CalculatorApplication
{
  class NumberManipulator
  {
```

```
public void getValues(out int x, out int y )
{
    Console.WriteLine("Enter the first value: ");
    x = Convert.ToInt32(Console.ReadLine());
    Console.WriteLine("Enter the second value: ");
    y = Convert.ToInt32(Console.ReadLine());
}
static void Main(string[] args)
{
    NumberManipulator n = new NumberManipulator();
    /* local variable definition */
    int a , b;
    /* calling a function to get the values */
    n.getValues(out a, out b);
    Console.WriteLine("After method call, value of a : {0}", a);
    Console.WriteLine("After method call, value of b : {0}", b);
    Console.ReadLine();
}
```

}
}

You will get the following result on executing the above example.

Enter the first value:

7

Enter the second value:

8

After method call, value of a : 7

After method call, value of b : 8

Chapter 9
Working with Arrays and Strings

As you are working with C#, it is certain that you will come across arrays and strings. In fact, you have already used arrays while learning about the for each loop. As for strings, they have been used in various examples in the book. It is now time to get to know these two a bit better.

Getting to Know Arrays

An array will store a sequential collection of different elements. The collection will have a fixed size, and all the elements will be of the same type. They are used for storing a collection of data. However, a better way of defining them would be to say that they are a collection of variables kept at contiguous memory locations.

Array saves us the trouble of declaring multiple individual variables. Instead, we just need to declare a single array variable and then place the values required for them. Therefore, we do not have to create a list of variables such as a0, a1, a2 and so on.

Instead, we create an array a and use a[0], a[1] and a[2] and so on.

Remember that a specific element present in the array is accessible by means of an index. In C#, all arrays will have contiguous memory locations. The lowest address will correspond to the first element of the array while the highest address belongs to the last element.

Declaring Arrays

In C#, if you wish to declare an array, you will have to make use of the following syntax.

datatype[] arrayName;

Each of the elements the syntax has been discussed as follows.

- the datatype is used in order to specify the datatype of the elements that will be present in the array.

- [] specifies the array's rank. The rank of an array defines the size of the array.

- arrayName is the name of this array.

Initializing Arrays

Remember that declaring the array will not initialize it in the memory. Only after the array variable has been initialized will you be able to assign values to it? As the array is a reference type, you will have to use the new keyword in order to create an instance of the given array.

The following example shows you how.

double[] balance = new double[10];

Assigning Values to the Array

It is possible to assign values to individual elements of the array. In order to do so, the index number of the element needs to be used. The following example illustrates this.

double[] balance = new double[10];

balance[0] = 4500.0;

Values can also be assigned to the array when it is being declared.

double[] balance = { 2340.0, 4523.69, 3421.0};

It is also possible to create and initialize the array at the same time.

int [] marks = new int[5] { 99, 98, 92, 97, 95};

If you want, you can exclude the array's size.

int [] marks = new int[] { 99, 98, 92, 97, 95};

An array variable can be copied into another array variable. In this case, the target, as well as the source array variable, will be pointing to the exact same memory location. The following example demonstrates this.

int [] marks = new int[] { 99, 98, 92, 97, 95};

int[] score = marks;

When an array is being created, the C# compiler will implicitly initialize all of its elements to a specific default value. The default value depends on the type of the array. For example, all elements in an int array will be initialized to 0.

Accessing the Elements in an Array

An element can be accessed by indexing the array name. In order to do so, the index of the required element can be placed inside square brackets after the array name. This is shown in the example below.

double salary = balance[9];

The example shown below will illustrate the concepts that you have learned so far about arrays. That is an assignment, declaration and accessing the elements.

using System;

namespace ArrayApplication

{

  class MyArray

```csharp
{
    static void Main(string[] args)
    {
        int [] n = new int[10]; /* n is an array of 10 integers */
        int i,j;
        /* initialize elements of array n */
        for ( i = 0; i < 10; i++ )
        {
            n[ i ] = i + 100;
        }
        /* output each array element's value */
        for (j = 0; j < 10; j++ )
        {
            Console.WriteLine("Element[{0}] = {1}", j, n[j]);
        }
        Console.ReadKey();
    }
}
```

}

After executing the code shown above, the following result will be produced.

Element[0] = 100

Element[1] = 101

Element[2] = 102

Element[3] = 103

Element[4] = 104

Element[5] = 105

Element[6] = 106

Element[7] = 107

Element[8] = 108

Element[9] = 109

Concepts Regarding Arrays in C#

When working with arrays in C#, there are a few important concepts which you should know about. They can prove to be useful in the advanced courses.

Multidimensional Arrays

C# provides support for multidimensional arrays. The most common and simplest form of these arrays is the 2-dimensional array.

Jagged Arrays

These arrays can be simply said to be arrays of arrays.

The Array Class

This class is defined in the System namespace. This is the base class for all the arrays. As such, it provides a number of methods and properties to help you while working with arrays.

Passing an Array to a Function

It is possible to pass a function to the array. This can be done by specifying the name of the array but without the index.

Param Arrays

They are used for passing an unknown number of parameters to a given function.

This concludes the section on arrays. Now, we will be taking a look at strings.

Introducing Strings

In C#, strings can be used as an array of characters. Be that as it may, the common procedure is using the string keyword for declaring a storing variable. You must remember that the string keyword is simply an alias for the class System.String.

Creation of a String Object

A string object can be created by any one of the following procedures.

- By getting a string literal assigned to a String variable
- With the use of a String class constructor
- Via the retrieval of property or by calling a method which can return a string.
- Through the use of the string concatenation operator, +
- By means of a call to a formatting method that can convert an object or value into the corresponding string representation.

The following example illustrates the creation of a string object.

using System;

namespace StringApplication

{

  class Program

  {

    static void Main(string[] args)

    {

```csharp
//from string literal and string concatenation
string fname, lname;
fname = "John";
lname = "Smith";
string fullname = fname + lname;
Console.WriteLine("Full Name: {0}", fullname);
//by using string constructor
char[] letters = { 'H', 'e', 'l', 'l','o' };
string greetings = new string(letters);
Console.WriteLine("Greetings: {0}", greetings);
//methods returning string
string[] sarray = { "Hello", "From", "The", "Earth" };
string message = String.Join(" ", sarray);
Console.WriteLine("Message: {0}", message);
//formatting method to convert a value
DateTime waiting = new DateTime(2016, 10, 10, 17, 58, 1);
string chat = String.Format("Message sent at {0:t} on {0:D}", waiting);
```

> Console.WriteLine("Message: {0}", chat);

   }

  }

 }

After compiling and executing the code shown above, the following result is produced.

Full Name: Rowan Atkinson

Greetings: Hello

Message: Hello From The Earth

Message: Message sent at 5:58 PM on Wednesday, October 10, 2016

String Class Properties

The String class possesses two properties. They are mentioned as follows.

- Chars: This gets the Char object at the position specified in the given String object.

- Length: This will get the total number of characters in the given String object.

Methods Present In the String Class

There are several methods available in the String class. These methods can be helpful when you are working with string objects. Here are some of the methods that are commonly used.

public static int Compare(string strA, string strB)

This will compare the two given string objects. An integer will be returned that indicates the relative position of the objects in the sort order.

public static int Compare(string strA, string strB, bool ignoreCase)

This will compare the two given string objects and will also return an integer indicating the relative position of the objects in the sort order. Be that as it may, it will be ignoring case when the Boolean parameter is true.

public static string Concat(string str0, string str1)

This will concatenate two string objects. It is possible to increase the number of string objects being concatenated.

public bool Contains(string value)

It will return a value that indicates whether the given String object is present in the given string.

public static string Copy(string str)

This will create a new String object that has the same value as the given string.

public bool EndsWith(string value)

This will determine if the end of the given string object is a match with the given string.

public static bool Equals(string a, string b)

This will determine if the two given String objects have the exact same value.

public int IndexOf(char value)

This will return the index of the given Unicode character in the string. The zero-based index will be provided of the first occurrence of the character.

public static string Format(string format, Object argo)

This will replace one or multiple format items in the given string. They will be replaced with the string representation of the given object.

public string Insert(int startIndex, string value)

This will return a new string that has a given string inserted at a specific index position in the given string object.

public static bool IsNullOrEmpty(string value)

This indicates if the given string is a null string or an empty string.

public static string Join(string separator, params string[] value)

This will concatenate all the elements of the string array by using the given separator between each of the elements in it.

public static string Join(string separator, string[] value, int startIndex, int count)

This will concatenate the stated elements of the string by using the given separator between each of the elements.

public int LastIndexOf(char value)

This returns the index position of the given Unicode character inside the current string object. The zero-based index position will be used, and only the last occurrence will be mentioned.

public string Remove(int startIndex)

This will remove all characters present in the current instance starting from the specified position. It will continue through till the last position. Finally, the string will be returned.

There is a wide range of other methods and constructors for the String class. The MSDN library contains the complete list. Now, let us take a look at a few examples that demonstrate how some of the methods given above can be used.

The example below illustrates how strings can be compared.

```
using System;

namespace StringApplication
{
  class StringProg
  {
    static void Main(string[] args)
    {
      string str1 = "This is test";
      string str2 = "This is text";
      if (String.Compare(str1, str2) == 0)
      {
        Console.WriteLine(str1 + " and " + str2 + " are equal.");
      }
      else
      {
```

```
            Console.WriteLine(str1 + " and " + str2 + " are not equal.");
        }
        Console.ReadKey() ;
    }
  }
}
```

On executing the code shown above, the following result will be produced.

This is a test, and This is text are not equal.

The example shown below demonstrates a string that contains another string.

```
using System;
namespace StringApplication
{
  class StringProg
  {
    static void Main(string[] args)
    {
```

```csharp
string str = "This is test";

if (str.Contains("test"))

{

    Console.WriteLine("The sequence 'test' was found.");

}

Console.ReadKey() ;
      }
   }
}
```

The following result is produced on executing the code shown above.

The sequence 'test' was found.

The example is given as follows how you can get a substring.

```csharp
using System;

namespace StringApplication

{

   class StringProg

   {
```

```
static void Main(string[] args)
{
    string str = "Last night I dreamt of San Pedro";
    Console.WriteLine(str);
    string substr = str.Substring(23);
    Console.WriteLine(substr);
}
  }
}
```

When the above code is compiled and executed, it produces the following result:

San Pedro

Joining Strings:

```
using System;
namespace StringApplication
{
  class StringProg
  {
```

```
static void Main(string[] args)
{
    string[] starray = new string[]{"Down the way nights are dark",
    "And the sun shines daily on the mountain top",
    "I took a trip on a sailing ship",
    "And when I reached Jamaica",
    "I made a stop"};
    string str = String.Join("\n", starray);
    Console.WriteLine(str);
}
}
}
```

The result produced after executing the code shown above is given as follows.

Down the way nights are dark

And the sun shines daily on the mountain top

I took a trip on a sailing ship

And when I reached Jamaica

I made a stop

With that, we have come to the end of arrays and strings. The information given here should be enough for most C# beginner grade projects.

Chapter 10
An Insight to Structures and Enums

Now that you have learned about arrays and strings, it is time to take a look at structures and enums. They play vital roles in a variety of programs. Therefore, let's find out more about them.

What is a Structure?

A structure in C# is a value type datatype. With it, it becomes possible for a single variable to hold related data of different datatypes. To create a structure, you have to use the struct keyword. Structures are typically used for representing a record.

Let us take library books as our example in understanding structures better. In a library, you will have to keep track of the books. Now, there are various attributes you may want to consider while tracking each book such as the title, the author, and the subject among others. We will be using this example in the programs in the following sections.

Defining Structures

As mentioned earlier, the struct statement has to be used for the defining structure. This statement can define a new datatype that has more than one member.

Let us take that example about the books and define a Book structure based on it. The following is how it will look like.

struct Books

{

  public string title;

  public string author;

  public string subject;

  public int book_id;

};

The example given below shows you how the structure is being used.

using System;

struct Books

{

  public string title;

```csharp
   public string author;
   public string subject;
   public int book_id;
};
public class testStructure
{
   public static void Main(string[] args)
   {
      Books Book1;   /* Declare Book1 of type Book */
      Books Book2;   /* Declare Book2 of type Book */
      /* book 1 specification */
      Book1.title = "C# Programming";
      Book1.author = "John Smith";
      Book1.subject = "C# Programming Tutorial";
      Book1.book_id = 123456;
      /* book 2 specification */
      Book2.title = "Java Programming";
      Book2.author = "Jane Smith";
```

```
Book2.subject = "Java Programming Tutorial";

Book2.book_id = 456789;

/* print Book1 info */

Console.WriteLine( "Book 1 title : {0}", Book1.title);

Console.WriteLine("Book 1 author : {0}", Book1.author);

Console.WriteLine("Book 1 subject : {0}", Book1.subject);

Console.WriteLine("Book 1 book_id :{0}", Book1.book_id);

/* print Book2 info */

Console.WriteLine("Book 2 title : {0}", Book2.title);

Console.WriteLine("Book 2 author : {0}", Book2.author);

Console.WriteLine("Book 2 subject : {0}", Book2.subject);

Console.WriteLine("Book 2 book_id : {0}", Book2.book_id);

Console.ReadKey();

   }

}
```

After compiling and executing the code shown above, the following result will be produced.

Book 1 title : C# Programming

Book 1 author : John Smith

Book 1 subject : C# Programming Tutorial

Book 1 book_id : 123456

Book 2 title : Java Programming

Book 2 author : Jane Smith

Book 2 subject : Java Programming Tutorial

Book 2 book_id : 456789

The Features of Structures in C#

In the above examples, you made use of a simple structure. If you have already worked with structures in C or C++, you should know that the structures in C# are rather different from what you find in either of those languages. The features of a structure in C# are given as follows.

- It is possible for structures to have fields, methods, properties, indexers, events and operator methods.

- They can have defined constructors. However, they cannot have destructors. At the same time, it is not possible to define a default constructor for the structure. Default constructors will be automatically defined. As such, they cannot be modified.

- Structures, unlike classes, cannot inherit from the other structures or classes.

- In the same way, it is not possible to use them as a base for the other classes or structures.

- You cannot specify structure members as virtual, abstract or protected.

- It is possible for structures to implement one or multiple interfaces.

- On creating a struct object with the New operator, it will get created, and the right constructor called. It is possible for struct objects to be instantiated without the use of the New operator, unlike classes.

- The fields will remain unassigned if you do not use the New operator. As a result, the object will be unusable till all you initialize all the fields.

The Difference between Classes and Structures

There are a few points of difference between these two. They are listed as follows.

- Structures are value types while classes are of the reference type.

- Inheritance is not supported by structures, unlike classes.

- Structures cannot have a default constructor.

Now that we know more about structures let us recreate the earlier example on the structure Books and get a better understanding.

using System;

struct Books

{

  private string title;

  private string author;

  private string subject;

  private int book_id;

  public void getValues(string t, string a, string s, int id)

  {

   title = t;

   author = a;

   subject = s;

   book_id = id;

  }

```csharp
   public void display()
   {
      Console.WriteLine("Title : {0}", title);
      Console.WriteLine("Author : {0}", author);
      Console.WriteLine("Subject : {0}", subject);
      Console.WriteLine("Book_id :{0}", book_id);
   }
};
public class testStructure
{
   public static void Main(string[] args)
   {
      Books Book1 = new Books();   /* Declare Book1 of type Book */
      Books Book2 = new Books();   /* Declare Book2 of type Book */

      /* book 1 specification */
      Book1.getValues("C# Programming",
```

"John Smith", "C# Programming Tutorial",123456);

/* book 2 specification */

Book2.getValues("Java Programming",

"Jane Smith", "Java Programming Tutorial", 456789);

/* print Book1 info */

Book1.display();

/* print Book2 info */

Book2.display();

Console.ReadKey();

　}

}

On executing the code above, the result will remain the same as shown below.

Title : C# Programming

Author : John Smith

Subject : C# Programming Tutorial

Book_id : 123456

Title : Java Programming

Author : Jane Smith

Subject : Java Programming Tutorial

Book_id : 456789

With that, the section on structures comes to an end. Now, let us take a look at enums.

What is Enums?

Enums are short for enumerations. An enumeration can be said to be a set of named integer constants. The enum keyword is used for declaring an enumerated type. In C#, enumerations are of the value datatype. As such, an enumeration will contain its own values. It is incapable of inheriting or passing inheritance.

Declaring an enum Variable

Generally, the syntax you need to follow to declare an enumeration is given below.

enum <enum_name>

{

　enumeration list

};

Take a look at what each of these elements means.

- **enum_name**: This specifies the name of the enumeration type.

- **enumeration list**: This is a list of identifiers, each of which is separated by commas.

In the enumeration list, each symbol represents an integer value. Each symbol will be greater than the one preceding it. The default value of the first symbol in an enumeration list will be 0.

The following example illustrates the use of enumeration variables.

using System;

namespace EnumApplication

{

  class EnumProgram

  {

    enum Days { Sun, Mon, tue, Wed, thu, Fri, Sat };

    static void Main(string[] args)

    {

      int WeekdayStart = (int)Days.Mon;

      int WeekdayEnd = (int)Days.Fri;

      Console.WriteLine("Monday: {0}", WeekdayStart);

      Console.WriteLine("Friday: {0}", WeekdayEnd);

Console.ReadKey();

   }

  }

}

After executing the code given above, the following result can be achieved.

Monday: 1

Friday: 5

Chapter 11

Becoming Familiar with the Concept of Inheritance

As mentioned in the previous chapter, one of the most important aspects of any object oriented programming language is classes. In the same way, inheritance is a key concept in object oriented programming.

As C# is such a language, you will have to utilize inheritance sooner than later. In fact, the entirety of the .NET framework has been built upon the concept of inheritance. It is responsible for the expression that everything is an object.

Inheritance, in simple terms, enables you to create classes that can inherit specific attributes from their parent classes. In C#, even a simple number can be an instance of a class that inherits from the parent class, System.Object.

Inheritance can be a bit advanced for some beginners. However, it is better to become familiar with it sooner than later because of the roles it plays in C# programming. Here is an example that illustrates the use of inheritance.

```csharp
public class Animal

{

    public void Greet()

    {

        Console.WriteLine ("Hello! I'm some kind of animal.");

    }

}

public class Cat: Animal

{

}
```

As you can see, an Animal class has been defined first along with a simple method that sends out a greeting to the user. This is followed up by defining a Cat class. We now use a colon to inform C# that the Cat class is going to be inheriting from the Animal class. Now, it is possible to start using these classes

```csharp
Animal animal = new Animal ();

animal.Greet ();
```

Dog dog = new Dog ();

dog.Greet ();

On running the example given above, you will find that the Greet () method is executed even though it has not been defined for the Cat class. This is because the method has been inherited by the Cat class from the Animal class.

Of course, the greeting given in the above examples are rather vague. It is possible to customize the greeting so that it contains the name of the animal. This is shown in the next example.

public class Animal

{

   public virtual void Greet()

   {

      Console.WriteLine ("Hello! I'm some kind of animal.");

   }

}

public class Cat: Animal

{

   public override void Greet()

    {

        Console.WriteLine ("Hello! I'm a cat.");

    }

}

As you can notice, there are a few changes to the code in the above examples. A method has been added on the Cat Class and, on the Animal class, the virtual keyword has been added to the method. Additionally, there is the presence of the override keyword on the Cat class.

In C#, it is not possible to override an item of any class unless it has been marked as virtual. It is certainly possible to keep accessing the inherited method even after it has been overridden with the help of the base keyword. This is shown in the example below.

public override void Greet()

{

   base.Greet ();

   Console.WriteLine ("Yes! I am - a cat!");

}

However, methods are not the only thing that can be inherited. In fact, nearly all members of a class will be inherited. This includes properties and fields. All you need to ensure the proper result is to utilize the proper visibility, as explained in the earlier chapter.

Another thing you need to remember is that inheritance need not take place from one class to another. It is possible to have an entire hierarchy of classes that inherit from one another. Keeping in tune with the earlier examples, it is possible to create a Kitten class that inherits from the Cat class and that, in turn, will be inheriting from the Animal class.

However, there is one thing that you cannot perform in C#, and that is multiple inheritances. In other words, you cannot make a class inherit from multiple classes simultaneously. C# does not support this feature.

Understanding the Concept of Base Class and Derived Class

It is possible for a class to be derived from more than a single class. As a result, it is possible to inherit the functions and data from multiple base classes.

Given below is the syntax used to create derived classes in C#.

<acess-specifier> class <base_class>

{

...

}

class <derived_class> : <base_class>

{

...

}

Let us take the help of an example to get a better understanding of base classes and derived classes. In the following example, Shape is the base class while Rectangle is its derived class.

using System;

namespace InheritanceApplication

{

  class Shape

  {

    public void setWidth(int w)

    {

      width = w;

    }

    public void setHeight(int h)

```
   {
      height = h;
   }
   protected int width;
   protected int height;
}
// Derived class
class Rectangle: Shape
{
   public int getArea()
   {
      return (width * height);
   }
}


class RectangleTester
{
   static void Main(string[] args)
```

```
   {
      Rectangle Rect = new Rectangle();
      Rect.setWidth(5);
      Rect.setHeight(7);
      // Print the area of the object.
      Console.WriteLine("Total area: {0}", Rect.getArea());
      Console.ReadKey();
   }
  }
}
```

On executing the code shown above, the following result can be achieved.

Total area: 35

Initialization of a Base Class

As you know, the derived class will inherit the member methods and member variables of the base class. As such, it is necessary to create the super class object before the creation of the subclass. Instructions for the initialization of the superclass can be provided in the member initialization list.

The following example illustrates this.

```csharp
using System;
namespace RectangleApplication
{
    class Rectangle
    {
        //member variables
        protected double length;
        protected double width;
        public Rectangle(double l, double w)
        {
            length = l;
            width = w;
        }
        public double GetArea()
        {
            return length * width;
        }
        public void Display()
```

```csharp
    {
        Console.WriteLine("Length: {0}", length);
        Console.WriteLine("Width: {0}", width);
        Console.WriteLine("Area: {0}", GetArea());
    }
}//end class Rectangle


class Tabletop : Rectangle
{
    private double cost;
    public Tabletop(double l, double w) : base(l, w)
    { }
    public double GetCost()
    {
        double cost;
        cost = GetArea() * 70;
        return cost;
    }
```

```csharp
    public void Display()
    {
        base.Display();
        Console.WriteLine("Cost: {0}", GetCost());
    }
}
class ExecuteRectangle
{
    static void Main(string[] args)
    {
        Tabletop t = new Tabletop(4.5, 7.5);
        t.Display();
        Console.ReadLine();
    }
}
```

After the above code has been executed, the following result is achieved.

Length: 4.5

Width: 7.5

Area: 33.75

Cost: 2362.5

C# and Multiple Inheritance

Multiple inheritances are not supported by C#. On the other hand, it is possible to use interfaces in order to implement multiple inheritances. This is demonstrated by the following example.

using System;

namespace InheritanceApplication

{

  class Shape

  {

    public void setWidth(int w)

    {

      width = w;

    }

    public void setHeight(int h)

```
   {
      height = h;
   }
   protected int width;
   protected int height;
}
// Base class PaintCost
public interface PaintCost
{
   int getCost(int area);
}


// Derived class
class Rectangle : Shape, PaintCost
{
   public int getArea()
   {
      return (width * height);
```

```
        }
    public int getCost(int area)
    {
        return area * 70;
    }
}
class RectangleTester
{
    static void Main(string[] args)
    {
        Rectangle Rect = new Rectangle();
        int area;
        Rect.setWidth(5);
        Rect.setHeight(7);
        area = Rect.getArea();
        // Print the area of the object.
        Console.WriteLine("Total area: {0}", Rect.getArea());
```

Console.WriteLine("Total paint cost: ${0}" , Rect.getCost(area));

Console.ReadKey();

}

}

}

The result produced after executing the code shown above is given as follows.

Total area: 35

Total paint cost: $2450

Chapter 12

Using Constructors and Destructors

In the book, you will have come across these two terms. Well, they are not difficult to grasp. Here, we will be taking a look at each of them in turn.

Constructors in C#

A class constructor can be said to be a special member function of the class. This will be executed whenever new objects are created by that class. A constructor will have the exact same name as its class. There are no return types for a constructor.

The following example demonstrates constructors.

using System;

namespace LineApplication

{

  class Line

  {

```
private double length;   // Length of a line

public Line()

{

   Console.WriteLine("Object is being created");

}

public void setLength( double len )

{

  length = len;

}

public double getLength()

{

  return length;

}

static void Main(string[] args)

{

   Line line = new Line();


   // set line length
```

line.setLength(6.0);

Console.WriteLine("Length of line : {0}", line.getLength());

Console.ReadKey();

   }

  }

}

On executing, the code should above, the following result is produced.

Object is being created

Length of line : 6

Parameterized Constructors

By default, a constructor will not have any parameters. Be that as it may, you can add parameters to your constructor. These constructors are known as parameterized constructors. With the help of this technique, you can assign an initial value to a specific object during its creation. The following example will show you how.

using System;

namespace LineApplication

```csharp
{
    class Line
    {
        private double length;   // Length of a line
        public Line(double len)  //Parameterized constructor
        {
            Console.WriteLine("Object is being created, length = {0}", len);
            length = len;
        }
        public void setLength( double len )
        {
            length = len;
        }
        public double getLength()
        {
            return length;
        }
```

```
static void Main(string[] args)
{
    Line line = new Line(10.0);
    Console.WriteLine("Length of line : {0}", line.getLength());
    // set line length
    line.setLength(6.0);
    Console.WriteLine("Length of line : {0}", line.getLength());
    Console.ReadKey();
  }
 }
}
```

The result produced on executing the code shown above is given as follows.

Object is being created; length = 10

Length of line : 10

Length of line : 6

Destructors in C#

Like constructors, a destructor is also a special member function of a class. However, it gets executed only when one of the objects of the class goes outside of its designated scope. The name of the destructor is the exact same as that of its class, but it will have a prefixed tilde (~) with it. A destructor is incapable of returning a value or taking any parameters. Destructors can be rather beneficial as they can release memory resources before the program is exited. It is not possible for destructors to be inherited.

The following example demonstrates the use of destructors.

using System;

namespace LineApplication

{

  class Line

  {

    private double length;   // Length of a line

    public Line() // constructor

    {

      Console.WriteLine("Object is being created");

    }

```csharp
~Line() //destructor
{
    Console.WriteLine("Object is being deleted");
}
public void setLength( double len )
{
    length = len;
}

public double getLength()
{
    return length;
}
static void Main(string[] args)
{
    Line line = new Line();
    // set line length
    line.setLength(6.0);
```

Console.WriteLine("Length of line : {0}", line.getLength());

  }

 }

}

On executing the code shown in the above example, the result produced is as follows.

Object is being created

Length of line : 6

Object is being deleted

Now you know what constructors and destructors are. You are certain to find them useful when you start writing complex programs. As such, make sure that you have a thorough understanding.

Chapter 13

Getting Into Interfaces and Polymorphism

These are two concepts that you should get familiarized with as early as possible. Trey will be helpful in the development of C# programs down the line.

Introducing Interfaces

An interface can be defined as the syntactical contract which is to be followed by all of the classes inheriting that interface. The interface will define the 'what' section of the contract. The deriving classes will be defining the 'how' section of the syntactical contract.

Interfaces will define the methods, properties, and events that are members of it. Another point to note is that the interfaces will contain the members' declaration only. The responsibility of defining the members is given to the deriving class. As a result, it ensures the presence of a standard structure that can be followed by the deriving classes.

Declaring an Interface

An interface can be declared with the interface keyword. In fact, it has similarities with the declaration of a class. By default, the interface statements will be public. The following example demonstrates how an interface is declared.

public interface ITransactions

{

  // interface members

  void showTransaction();

  double getAmount();

}

Let us now take an example to understand how the above interface can be implemented.

using System.Collections.Generic;

using System.Linq;

using System.Text;

using System;

namespace InterfaceApplication

{

```csharp
public interface ITransactions
{
    // interface members
    void showTransaction();
    double getAmount();
}
public class Transaction : ITransactions
{
    private string tCode;
    private string date;
    private double amount;
    public Transaction()
    {
        tCode = " ";
        date = " ";
        amount = 0.0;
    }
    public Transaction(string c, string d, double a)
```

```
    {
        tCode = c;
        date = d;
        amount = a;
    }
    public double getAmount()
    {
        return amount;
    }
    public void showTransaction()
    {
        Console.WriteLine("Transaction: {0}", tCode);
        Console.WriteLine("Date: {0}", date);
        Console.WriteLine("Amount: {0}", getAmount());
    }
}
class Tester
{
```

```
static void Main(string[] args)
{
    Transaction t1 = new Transaction("001", "8/10/2012", 78900.00);
    Transaction t2 = new Transaction("002", "9/10/2012", 451900.00);
    t1.showTransaction();
    t2.showTransaction();
    Console.ReadKey();
}
    }
}
```

On executing the code shown above, the following result is produced.

Transaction: 001

Date: 8/10/2012

Amount: 78900

Transaction: 002

Date: 9/10/2012

Amount: 451900

Starting With Polymorphism

Literally, polymorphism can be defined as having multiple forms. However, in the object oriented programming methodology, polymorphism is generally described as having one interface but multiple functions. Now, polymorphism can be either static or dynamic.

Static Polymorphism

Static binding is the mechanism by which a function is linked with an object while the program is being compiled. In other words, the decision is taken during compile time. In C#, there are two techniques by which static polymorphism can be implemented.

- Function overloading
- Operator overloading

The following example demonstrates function overloading.

The following example shows using function print() to print different data types:

using System;

namespace PolymorphismApplication

{

```csharp
class Printdata
{
    void print(int i)
    {
        Console.WriteLine("Printing int: {0}", i );
    }
    void print(double f)
    {
        Console.WriteLine("Printing float: {0}" , f);
    }
    void print(string s)
    {
        Console.WriteLine("Printing string: {0}", s);
    }
    static void Main(string[] args)
    {
        Printdata p = new Printdata();
        // Call print to print integer
```

```
        p.print(5);

        // Call print to print float

        p.print(500.263);

        // Call print to print string

        p.print("Hello C++");

        Console.ReadKey();

    }

  }

}
```

On executing the code shown above, the following result is achieved.

Printing int: 5

Printing float: 500.263

Printing string: Hello C++

Dynamic Polymorphism

In this kind of polymorphism, the decision will be taken at the run time. This is implemented by means of method overriding.

With method overriding, it is possible to have methods in the derived and base classes with the same parameters and the same name. As a result, it becomes possible to point to a derived class through a base class's object at runtime.

The following example illustrates the use of dynamic polymorphism.

```
using System;

namespace PolymorphismApplication
{
  class Shape
  {
    protected int width, height;
    public Shape( int a=0, int b=0)
    {
      width = a;
      height = b;
    }
    public virtual int area()
    {
      Console.WriteLine("Parent class area :");
      return 0;
```

       }
   }
   class Rectangle: Shape
   {
      public Rectangle(int a=0, int b=0): base(a, b)
      {
      }
      public override int area ()
      {
         Console.WriteLine("Rectangle class area :");
         return (width * height);
      }
   }
   class Triangle: Shape
   {
      public Triangle(int a = 0, int b = 0): base(a, b)
      {
      }

```
public override int area()
{
    Console.WriteLine("Triangle class area :");
    return (width * height / 2);
}
}
class Caller
{
    public void CallArea(Shape sh)
    {
        int a;
        a = sh.area();
        Console.WriteLine("Area: {0}", a);
    }
}
class Tester
{
    static void Main(string[] args)
```

{

   Caller c = new Caller();

   Rectangle r = new Rectangle(10, 7);

   Triangle t = new Triangle(10, 5);

   c.CallArea(r);

   c.CallArea(t);

   Console.ReadKey();

}

}

}

The result produced after compiling and executing the code shown above is given below.

Rectangle class area:

Area: 70

Triangle class area:

Area: 25

This concludes the chapter on interfaces and polymorphism. Do not worry about using them at the moment. Strengthen your base in C# first.

Chapter 14
Learning the Basics of Debugging

Even if you have but a slight idea about computer programming, you should have heard about debugging. This is a vital process for all kinds of software and application programming. You see, there can be errors present in a program. These errors can be as simple as a typing mistake or an incorrect statement. They are all termed as bugs, and they can prevent your program from executing correctly. Therefore these bugs need to be removed, and that is achieved through debugging.

When you are writing simple applications of a few lines such as the examples shown in this book, it is quite easy for you to recognize the errors. You can simply execute the program and find out the bugs. However, with time, you will surely start writing more complex codes that are around hundreds of lines long and filled with complicated statements. Due to the high level of complexity involved, it becomes very difficult to determine the bugs.

In these situations, debugging becomes an extremely useful tool. As a result, you must take your time to understand this tool to become a better programmer. Without it, it is nearly impossible to correct the bugs you can find in the complex code.

Understanding Print Debugging

The most common type of debugging used is known as print debugging. Although it is the most basic kind of debugging, it is often used by advanced programmers due to its effectiveness in certain situations.

In print debugging, the application is made to print a number or text. This allows you to find out which sections of the code have been executed and what are contained in the variables. In C#, the Console.Write () method can be used for printing a status message or for displaying the contents of a specific variable on the console.

For a few situations, this will be enough. On the other hand, you will have much better tools to use when you are using a good IDE such as Visual Studio or even the Express versions. The good thing is that they are quite easy to use once know the basic principles.

Introduction to the Breakpoint

The breakpoint is the first thing that you need to learn about debugging. As the name suggests, a breakpoint marks a specific point in the code where its execution will be taking a break. The application will not be rendered useless. Instead, the breakpoint simply pause the execution of the application.

If you are using Visual Studio or even the Express version, it is quite easy to implement breakpoints. In those IDEs, you will notice that there is a gray area located on the left hand side of the code. This is known as the gutter, and a left click on this area will cause a red circle to appear. This will be the breakpoint, and the debugger will stop the execution of the application at this point.

These are just the basics of debugging. As you advance as a C# programmer, you will automatically come to know about the various other kinds of debugging tools and methods apart from the most complicated aspects of debugging.

Chapter 15
Tips for C# Beginners

Like all programming languages, C# has its own nuances and features. As a result, it is easy for a beginner to feel overwhelmed with the language. For this reason, here are a few tips that can help you overcome some of the problems you face as a beginner and take the next step into becoming a full-fledged C# programmer.

Keep Practicing

Nobody becomes an expert in anything overnight. This is most certainly true of computer programming. It will certainly take a lot of time to develop the skills and procure the knowledge required for calling yourself an expert. As such, you should remain patient and keep practicing C#. At the same time, you should keep practicing a variety of tasks within C#.

Don't Get Hung Up

This is quite a common problem with programmers, even those at the advanced level. The fact is there is rarely one best way of doing things in an object oriented programming language like

C#. Therefore, you should not get fixated on a particular process or technique. It is certainly possible that there are other processes which work better.

Strengthen Your Base

You may learn to write code, but you must also know how each concept or function comes together to make the code work. In other words, you need to understand the fundamentals and the basics thoroughly. This will enable to you understand why a piece of code works in the way it does and what possible bugs are leading to the problem in the execution. Therefore, you will become a better developer.

Learn Some Advanced Ideas Extensively

Of course, you shouldn't expect to master all the advanced techniques and ideas in C# within a few months of starting it. However, it will help your progress greatly if you take the time to learn a few concepts in detail. You should become really good in working with those few concepts. You are free to choose which concepts you want to concentrate on. They can be something that you come across more often during your work or something that interests you greatly. Trying to become an expert in few techniques is easier than trying to master all of them.

Take a Look at Code Written By Senior Programmers

One of the best ways to learn the concepts and techniques in C# is looking at the codes written by more experienced programmers. If you are working somewhere, you can easily ask the senior programmers to show you their code. Don't forget to understand why they used a particular technique and how they used it. Alternatively, you can browse through open source projects online. They may not necessarily be topnotch programmers, but you can still learn a lot. Of course, you must avoid blindly imitating what others are doing. Simply understand the idea and try to use it in your own code.

Conclusion

This marks the end of the book. You now possess the knowledge of the fundamentals of the object oriented programming language known as C#. You have also learned how to write some basic programs in this language and also what you need to start writing.

You can now start using some basic statements and methods in your code. Of course, you have learned how you can declare and define variables. More importantly, you know how you can create classes and even implement inheritance in them to create a hierarchy of code blocks. If you want, you can also start implementing conditional logic in your codes to make it a bit more advanced especially with the help of loops and multiple classes.

The information that you have gleaned from this book will be enough to help you get started with C# programming. Of course, there is a lot more to know and learn. Being a popular programming language, it is continually updated on a regular basis. As such, there will always be something new and exciting to learn. After becoming good at this programming language, you can easily start other incredible languages such as C or even Java and Ruby. You can even take a step into web development as C# is a part of the .NET framework.

I heartily thank you for selecting this book, and I hope that it has been useful for you. I also hope that you have been able to form a strong base from which you can launch C# as your career or hobby. Wishing you all the very best for your progress in C# and the future!

Want to Learn more about Programming?

Check out the other books by Joseph Connor:

- **Newest release (Oct, 2016):** Programming: Computer Programming For Beginners: Learn The Basics Of HTML5, JavaScript, & CSS or click the link https://www.amazon.com/dp/B01LYZGZKN

- Python: The Definitive Guide to Learning Python Programming for Beginners or click the link https://www.amazon.com/dp/B013NLBA9C

- Raspberry Pi 2: The Definitive Beginner's Guide to Get Started with Raspberry Projects or click the link https://www.amazon.com/dp/B013NKMD2Q

- Hacking: Hacking for Beginners - Computer Virus, Cracking, Malware, IT Security or click the link https://www.amazon.com/dp/B010K7BVOQ

- **The Amazon Bestseller:** Programming: Computer Programming for Beginners: Learn the Basics of Java, SQL & C++ - 3. Edition or click the link https://www.amazon.com/Programming-Computer-Beginners-Basics-JavaScript-ebook/dp/B014361TOM

Check out our Facebook and Instagram to receive updates on the newest releases!

Printed in Poland
by Amazon Fulfillment
Poland Sp. z o.o., Wrocław